ROTHERHAM PUBLIC LIBRARIES

TELL ME ABOUT

EXPLORERS
& FARAWAY PLACES

CHRISTOPHER MAYNARD

Kingfisher Books

Editor: Veronica Pennycook
Series designer: Terry Woodley
Designer: David West Children's Book Design
Illustrators: Chris Forsey (pp. 7, 10–17, 22–3, 26–7, 30–1, 34–7); Ross Watton (pp. 2–3, 18–21, 24–5, 28–9, 38); Adam Hook (pp. 4–5, 8–9, 32–3).
Inset illustrations: Kuo Kang Chen
Cover illustration: Chris Forsey

Kingfisher Books, Grisewood & Dempsey Ltd, Elsley House, 24–30 Great Titchfield Street, London W1P 7AD

First published in 1993 by Kingfisher Books
10 9 8 7 6 5 4 3 2 1
Copyright © Grisewood & Dempsey Ltd 1993

BRITISH LIBRARY CATALOGUING IN PUBLICATION DATA
A catalogue record for this book is available from the British Library

Hardback ISBN 1 85697 093 0
Paperback ISBN 1 85697 094 9

Phototypeset by Southern Positives and Negatives (SPAN), Lingfield, Surrey
Printed and bound in Spain

Contents

Who first explored by sea?

The first sea expeditions that we know about were made by the Ancient Egyptians. About 3500 years ago, the ruler of Egypt was Queen Hatshepsut. She sent a fleet of five large ships and a crew of 250 men to the Land of Punt at the southern end of the Red Sea.

The Land of Punt

Punt means 'land of incense', from the aromatic plants that grow there. Today, this region is called the Horn of Africa.

The Ancient Egyptian expedition landed somewhere along the coast of modern Somalia.

The Egyptians wanted to trade. They brought jewels and glass beads which they hoped to exchange for gold, elephant tusks, and the perfume known as incense.

ARABIA

ANCIENT EGYPT

RED SEA

River Nile

LAND OF PUNT

In the Land of Punt, the expedition came across a nation of dark-skinned people who lived in raised huts set on stilts.

DO YOU KNOW

About 2600 years ago, King Necho II of Egypt sent out a fleet to sail around Africa. The ships left from the Red Sea, heading south. Three years later they came back, claiming to be the first ever to have made this journey. But there is no proof that the ships really did make it.

The Egyptians' wooden ships could go almost anywhere. In calm weather the ships were rowed, but they could also sail with the wind. Their flat bottoms made it easy to land close to shore.

SAILING BY STARLIGHT

The very first sailors steered by the pattern of stars in the sky.

In the northern sky, the most useful star is the Pole Star because it shows where North lies. First, look for the group of stars known as the Plough. The two stars that form the outer edge of the Plough point straight

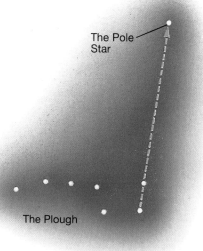

The Pole Star

The Plough

towards the Pole Star. The Pole Star hangs over the North Pole.

The southern sky does not have any one star that is bright enough to be easily spotted. Instead, find the Southern Cross. Imagine a line down the cross, add four and a half times its length, and you'll be looking directly over the South Pole.

Why did early explorers use maps?

Early explorers began to use maps because they were the best way to picture the world. They showed where rivers, mountains, islands and seas were to be found. They made it possible to find out what other explorers had already discovered. As maps became more accurate, they began to show distances between places. This helped explorers work out how far they had to travel.

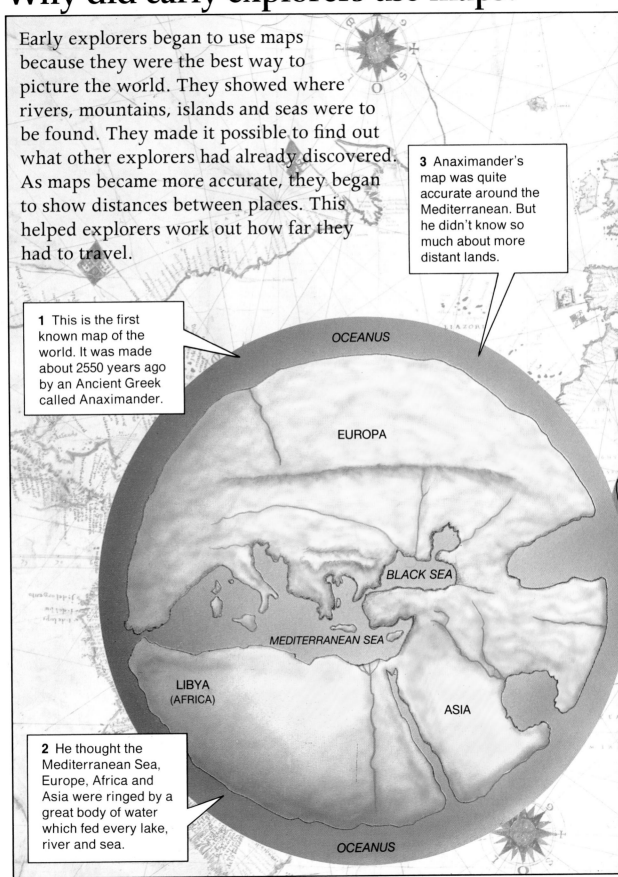

3 Anaximander's map was quite accurate around the Mediterranean. But he didn't know so much about more distant lands.

1 This is the first known map of the world. It was made about 2550 years ago by an Ancient Greek called Anaximander.

OCEANUS

EUROPA

BLACK SEA

MEDITERRANEAN SEA

LIBYA (AFRICA)

ASIA

2 He thought the Mediterranean Sea, Europe, Africa and Asia were ringed by a great body of water which fed every lake, river and sea.

OCEANUS

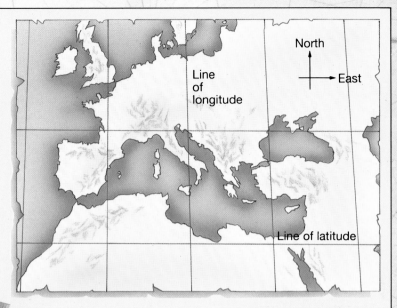

DO YOU KNOW

The first person to make maps that were really useful was the astronomer Ptolemy in the 2nd century AD. He drew maps with North at the top and East to the right. He used lines called latitude and longitude to plot the position of 9000 places in the ancient world.

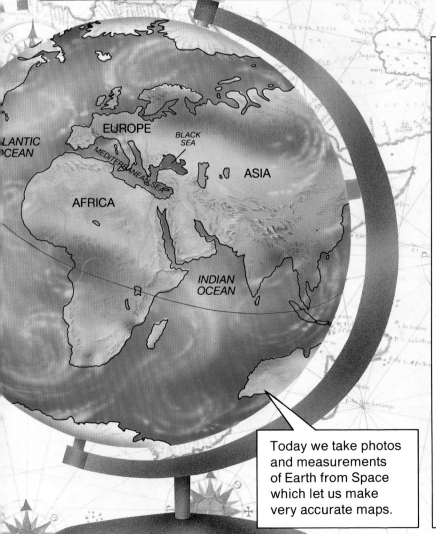

Today we take photos and measurements of Earth from Space which let us make very accurate maps.

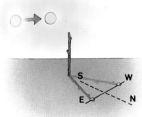

FINDING EAST AND WEST

1 Poke a stick into flat ground. Mark the tip of its shadow with a stone. Half an hour later mark the new shadow position with another stone.

2 The path between the two stones is an East-West line. The first stone marks the West, the second the East. A North-South line can be drawn too.

7

What helped explorers find their way?

The invention of the compass helped explorers to find their way much more accurately. A compass needle is pulled by the magnetic attraction of the North and South poles so that it always settles to point in a North-South direction. Using a compass, explorers could now steer a direct path from one part of the world to another.

 DO YOU KNOW

The needle of an Ancient Chinese compass would be magnetized, or made to point North, by being stroked against a lump of iron rock called a lodestone.

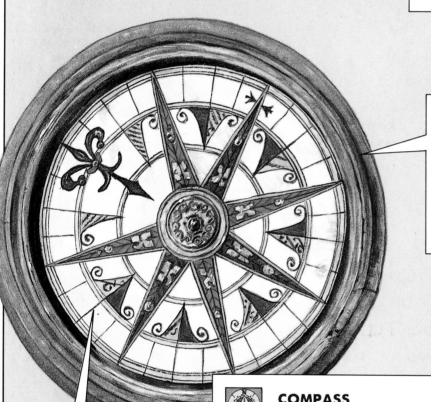

1 In the 1300s, the Italians invented the compass card. It had 32 points of direction marked on it, which made it much easier for an explorer to work out his exact direction.

2 The compass card was balanced on the point of a needle. Magnets were attached underneath the card. These magnets caused the whole card to swing on the needle to always point North.

COMPASS FACTS

● The Chinese discovered the magnetic compass as early as 200 BC. At first, only fortune tellers used it. Later, people realized it was also a good way to find the direction of North and South.

8

How did explorers steer by the stars?

Explorers could tell where they were heading by studying the position of the Sun or stars. The trick was to measure how high the Sun or stars were above the horizon. One instrument for doing this was the quadrant. It was first used in Europe around the early 1200s.

The quadrant was a quarter circle made out of metal. Degrees were marked along the rounded edge. A small weight called a plumb hung straight down from the squared-off corner.

The navigator would aim the quadrant at a well-known star. He would read off the degree where the plumb was hanging. He then worked out his latitude.

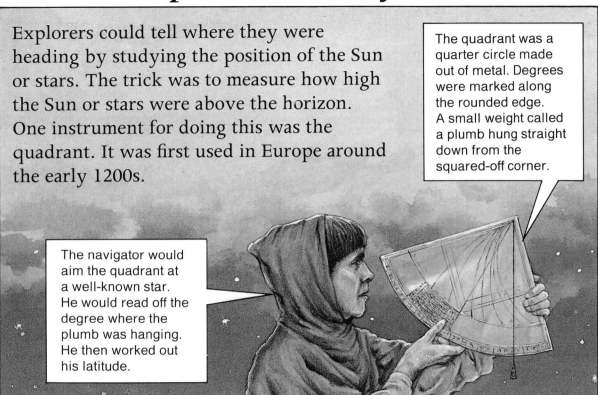

How did sailors measure their speed?

Sailors used a log to measure how fast their ship was going. This was a block of wood that was thrown into the water behind the ship. A line attached to the log unreeled as the ship moved.

Sailors noted the amount of line that ran out in a certain time and could then work out the ship's speed.

Who was the greatest explorer of all?

Ibn Battuta was one of the great explorers of all times. At the age of twenty he left his home in Tangiers to go to the holy city of Mecca. He returned when he was fifty, having travelled more than 100,000 kilometres around the world. During his voyages he had the most amazing adventures. He explored Africa, India, Sumatra and China. While he was an ambassador for the Sultan of Delhi he made a fortune, and then lost it. Finally, he wrote a book about his travels that made him famous.

1 Ibn Battuta left Tangiers in 1325 and spent the next 30 years exploring the world. This map shows some of the many places that he visited.

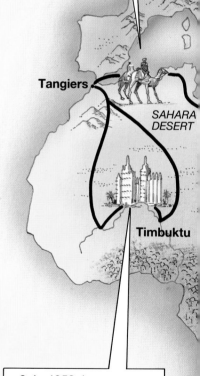

Tangiers

SAHARA DESERT

Timbuktu

 ARAB SAILORS

● Arab sailors like Ibn Battuta were the greatest travellers of their time. They were able to navigate their ships out of sight of land by using charts to plot latitude. They used an early kind of log to measure speed.

● Long before anyone else, Arab sailors voyaged across the Indian Ocean from Africa to India and on to Java.

● Arab travellers used ships called dhows. These had triangular sails which made them easier to sail than European ships.

9 In 1352, he explored the Sahara Desert. In Timbuktu he saw men with veiled faces and was upset by a local custom – women walked about in the nude! In 1355 he came home to Tangiers.

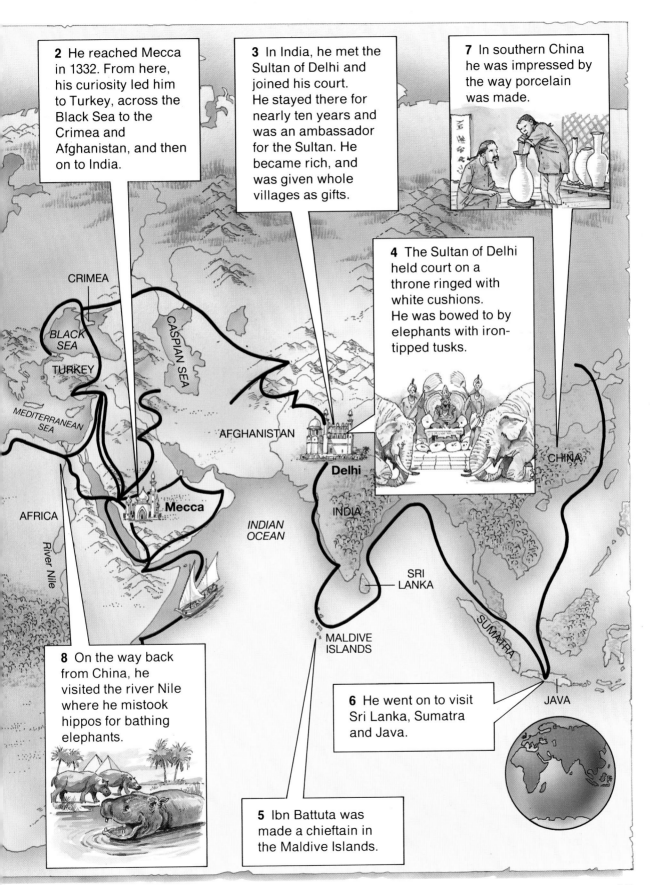

2 He reached Mecca in 1332. From here, his curiosity led him to Turkey, across the Black Sea to the Crimea and Afghanistan, and then on to India.

3 In India, he met the Sultan of Delhi and joined his court. He stayed there for nearly ten years and was an ambassador for the Sultan. He became rich, and was given whole villages as gifts.

7 In southern China he was impressed by the way porcelain was made.

4 The Sultan of Delhi held court on a throne ringed with white cushions. He was bowed to by elephants with iron-tipped tusks.

8 On the way back from China, he visited the river Nile where he mistook hippos for bathing elephants.

6 He went on to visit Sri Lanka, Sumatra and Java.

5 Ibn Battuta was made a chieftain in the Maldive Islands.

CRIMEA

BLACK SEA

CASPIAN SEA

TURKEY

MEDITERRANEAN SEA

AFGHANISTAN

Delhi

CHINA

AFRICA

Mecca

INDIAN OCEAN

INDIA

River Nile

SRI LANKA

MALDIVE ISLANDS

SUMATRA

JAVA

What was the Silk Route?

The Silk Route was a set of trails that led thousands of kilometres across Central Asia. From 500 BC to around AD 1650, the Silk Route was the main link between East and West. Along it, news about the wealth and glory of China trickled back to the Arab world and Europe. So, too, did rare and precious objects such as silk, pearls and porcelain. The travellers who made their way along the Silk Route to China were usually traders hoping to make their fortune.

Much of the land the Silk Route crossed was desert. In summer, the desert heat killed people and animals alike. Without the oasis towns on the fringes of the deserts, there would have been no lifeline to make the journey possible.

 OASIS FACTS

- An oasis is a place in a desert where there is water and plant life.

- In many oasis towns on the Silk Route it was so hot in summer that people had to live underground.

- The people in the oasis towns on the Silk Route grew wheat, cotton, melons and grapes, and kept sheep and horses. They made a good living by supplying the traders and travellers who were making their way along the Silk Route.

High mountain passes often filled with snow and stopped travellers from crossing for weeks at a time.

Traders mostly used camels because they could carry heavy loads, they would keep going for days with little water, and they could bear the heat and dust.

DO YOU KNOW

In 1931, 14 Citroën trucks set out along the Silk Route that camel caravans had once used. This expedition struggled from Beirut to Beijing, meeting bandits, washed out roads, stony deserts and icy mountains.

MONGOLIA

Samarkand

GOBI DESERT

TIBET

Beijing

INDIA

HIMALAYAS

CHINA

The Silk Route

The Silk Route was so very tough to travel along because it crossed some of the most dry and rugged areas of wilderness on Earth. It was also extremely long. The trek from Beijing to Samarkand took about six months.

Who was Marco Polo?

Marco Polo was a trader from Venice, in Italy. At the age of seventeen, he journeyed halfway around the world with his father and uncle to the court of Kublai Khan, the great ruler of China. The three Polos followed the ancient Silk Route that crossed the deserts and high mountains of Central Asia. They finally met Kublai Khan in 1275, four years after setting off from Venice.

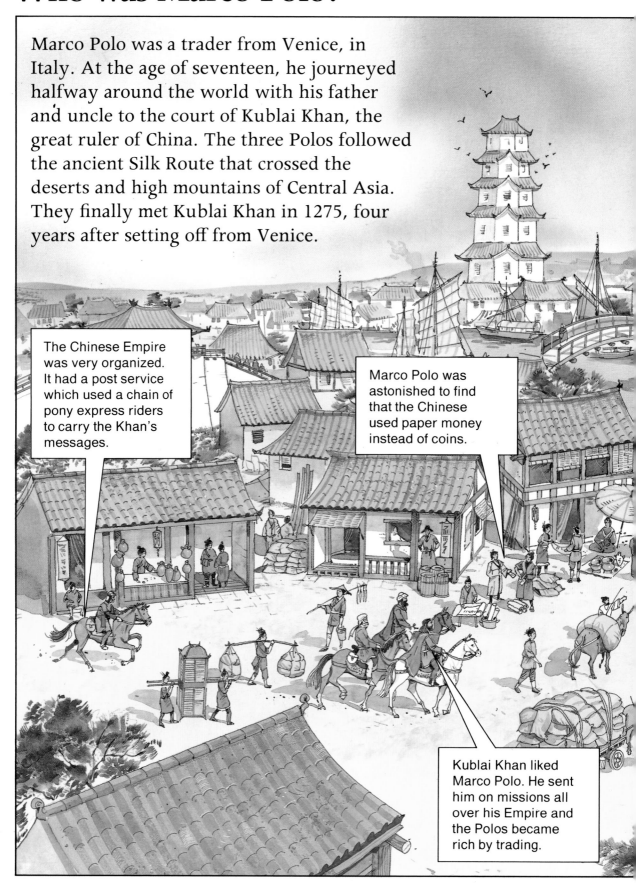

The Chinese Empire was very organized. It had a post service which used a chain of pony express riders to carry the Khan's messages.

Marco Polo was astonished to find that the Chinese used paper money instead of coins.

Kublai Khan liked Marco Polo. He sent him on missions all over his Empire and the Polos became rich by trading.

The ports were full of boats. Marco Polo was amazed by the many diamonds and pearls he saw being traded there.

Traders brought goods on camels from faraway Russia and Baghdad, in Iraq, to supply the busy Chinese markets.

 COURT FACTS

● Kublai Khan was so wealthy that he held banquets for 40,000 guests at a time.

● He kept astrologers on the roof of his palace to chant away clouds.

● Whenever the Khan took a drink, everyone in his company kneeled and a band played until he put his glass down.

● When the Great Khan took Marco Polo out hunting, 10,000 men were employed to look out for game.

● The Khan's winter court was in Beijing, the capital city. Marco Polo had never seen anywhere so splendid. The city was laid out in squares like a chessboard, and the streets were so straight he could see from one side of the city to the other.

What was the Age of Exploration?

In the 1400s, sailors from Europe started to hunt for new routes to the Far East, hoping to get rich by trading with China. Over the following 300 years most of the world was visited and mapped. This period is known as the Age of Exploration.

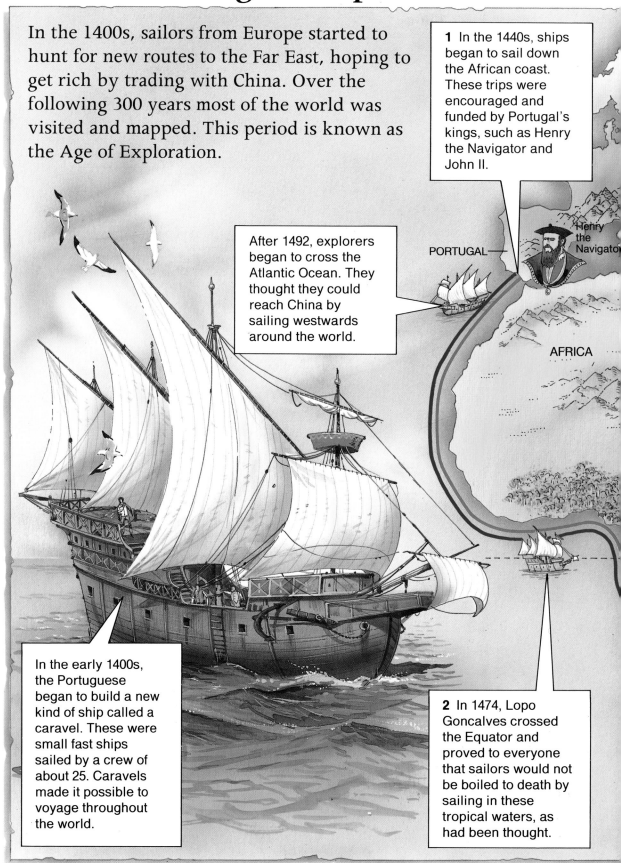

1 In the 1440s, ships began to sail down the African coast. These trips were encouraged and funded by Portugal's kings, such as Henry the Navigator and John II.

After 1492, explorers began to cross the Atlantic Ocean. They thought they could reach China by sailing westwards around the world.

PORTUGAL

Henry the Navigator

AFRICA

In the early 1400s, the Portuguese began to build a new kind of ship called a caravel. These were small fast ships sailed by a crew of about 25. Caravels made it possible to voyage throughout the world.

2 In 1474, Lopo Goncalves crossed the Equator and proved to everyone that sailors would not be boiled to death by sailing in these tropical waters, as had been thought.

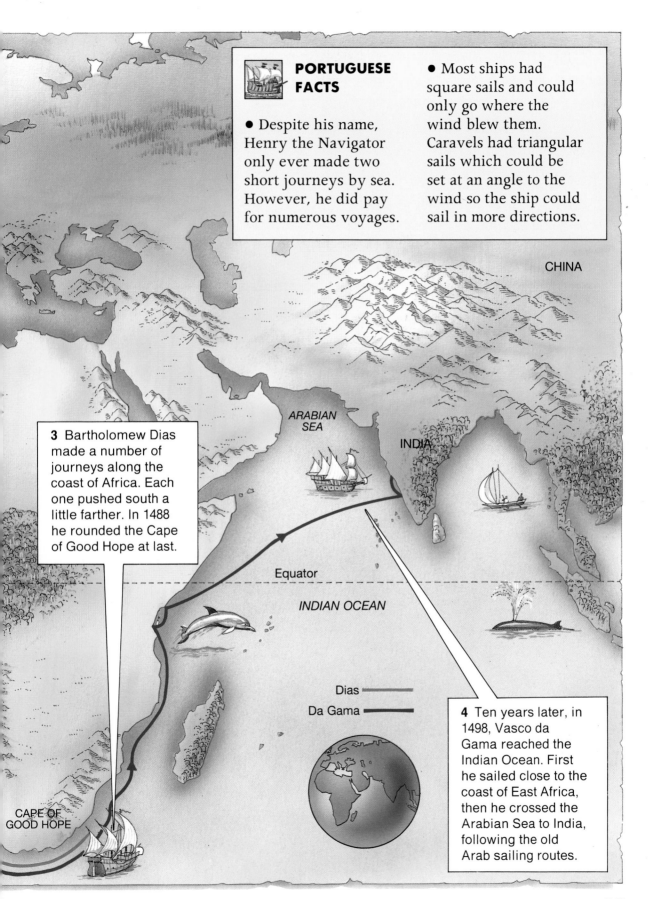

PORTUGUESE FACTS

● Despite his name, Henry the Navigator only ever made two short journeys by sea. However, he did pay for numerous voyages.

● Most ships had square sails and could only go where the wind blew them. Caravels had triangular sails which could be set at an angle to the wind so the ship could sail in more directions.

CHINA

ARABIAN SEA

INDIA

3 Bartholomew Dias made a number of journeys along the coast of Africa. Each one pushed south a little farther. In 1488 he rounded the Cape of Good Hope at last.

Equator

INDIAN OCEAN

Dias ━━━━
Da Gama ━━━━

4 Ten years later, in 1498, Vasco da Gama reached the Indian Ocean. First he sailed close to the coast of East Africa, then he crossed the Arabian Sea to India, following the old Arab sailing routes.

CAPE OF GOOD HOPE

Who was Christopher Columbus?

Christopher Columbus was the first person to return to Europe with news of the land that became known as America.

In 1492 he led three Spanish ships across the Atlantic Ocean on a voyage he thought would take him to China. When he got to America he had no idea that China was still half a world away. He was sure the islands he had reached, the Bahamas, were part of the coast of Asia.

Columbus led a fleet of three ships and 120 men. His biggest ship, the *Santa Maria*, was 39 metres long.

The only person with a private cabin was Columbus, aboard the *Santa Maria*. It was the only one of the three ships to have an upper deck.

There was just enough room to carry water for drinking, so nobody could wash for the 37 days the ships were at sea.

On 12 October, 1492, 37 days after leaving the Canary Islands, a sailor on the *Pinta* sighted a low-lying island that is part of the chain we call the Bahamas.

DO YOU KNOW

Columbus was not the first person to visit America. Around the year 1000, the Viking Leif Eriksson was blown off course on his way to Greenland. He landed in Newfound-

A Viking longship

land, but news of his discovery did not reach Europe.

Two of the ships, the *Nina* and the *Pinta*, had single decks open to the weather. The crew took turns to sleep curled up on deck.

NORTH AMERICA

SPAIN

CANARY ISLANDS

BAHAMAS

ATLANTIC OCEAN

AFRICA

SOUTH AMERICA

Crossing the Atlantic

Columbus was clever. Although he crossed the Atlantic Ocean at its widest point, he took a route where strong winds called the trade winds blow for most of the year. Later trips proved that this was indeed the fastest way from Europe to America.

Who explored North America?

Dozens of ships soon followed Columbus. While Spanish expeditions mostly went to Central and South America, French and English ones explored North America – all the time hunting for a way to China.

Jacques Cartier was a French sea captain who made three trips in the 1530s. He sailed up the St Lawrence River as far as Montreal, where his way was blocked by rapids. Instead of a shortcut to China, he found himself in a vast new land covered with forests as far as the eye could see.

Cartier arrived from France with three ships and 110 men. He had instructions from the King of France to search westward for a land rich in gold.

The Indians at Quebec welcomed Cartier warmly on his second trip, in 1535.

 LIFE AT SEA FACTS

- Mouldy biscuits and pickled pork and beef was the main food served at sea. Maggots sometimes had to be picked out of the biscuits before they were eaten.

- Food was cooked on an iron box set on a bed of sand towards the front of the ship.

- Ships were full of lice, cockroaches and rats.

- Officers usually slept in bunks. Sailors had to bed down on deck.

- Crews had to bring along their own clothes for the trip.

- The men drank beer and cider since few of them trusted fresh water.

- Many sailors went exploring in the hope of getting rich quick.

Cartier hoped the St Lawrence River was a way through North America. But it led him south to the five Great Lakes that lie at the heart of the continent. Here was a land rich with furs and timber, not gold.

? DO YOU KNOW

Explorers from Europe who came looking for a way to the Far East had no idea how big the world really was. Although they had crossed the Atlantic, they would need to go three times as far again to reach China.

CHINA   AMERICA

Cartier's Travels

Cartier took his smallest ship, the *Petit Hermine*, upriver as far as Montreal, looking for a route to China. He found North America to be a vast land, many times bigger than anyone had ever imagined.

As for the King of France, he was annoyed that Cartier had returned without any gold.

Cartier (1535)

Cartier (1534)

CANADA

Quebec

Montreal

Great Lakes

St Lawrence River

ATLANTIC OCEAN

What is the Northwest Passage?

Early explorers thought there might be an easy sea route around the northern end of America. They called it the Northwest Passage, and hoped it would be a way to the silks, spices and jewels of the East.

From 1576 onwards, expeditions spent over sixty years hunting for a way through the Arctic. All were defeated. Although a difficult route to the East did exist, it was not until 1906 that anyone sailed it.

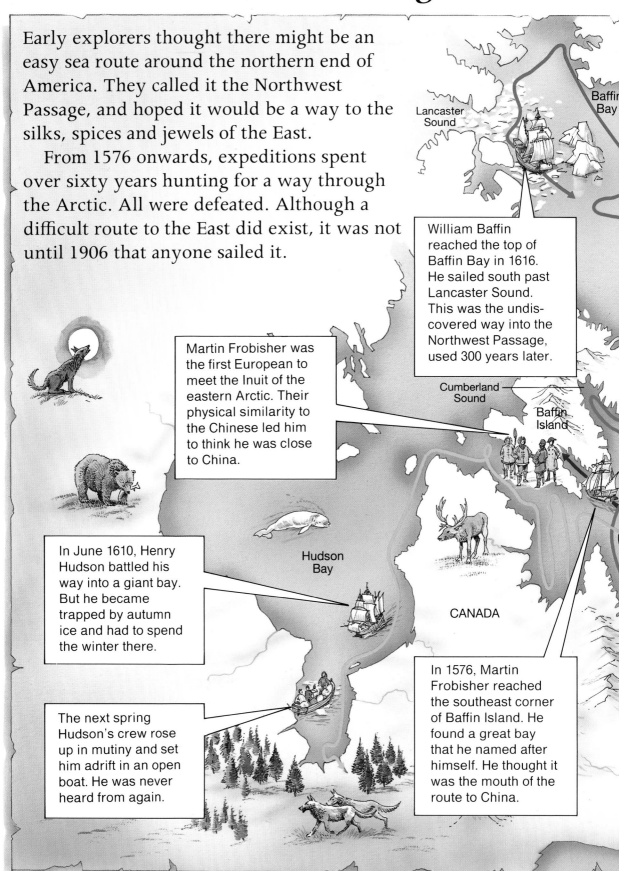

Baffin Bay

Lancaster Sound

William Baffin reached the top of Baffin Bay in 1616. He sailed south past Lancaster Sound. This was the undis-covered way into the Northwest Passage, used 300 years later.

Cumberland Sound

Baffin Island

Martin Frobisher was the first European to meet the Inuit of the eastern Arctic. Their physical similarity to the Chinese led him to think he was close to China.

In June 1610, Henry Hudson battled his way into a giant bay. But he became trapped by autumn ice and had to spend the winter there.

Hudson Bay

CANADA

The next spring Hudson's crew rose up in mutiny and set him adrift in an open boat. He was never heard from again.

In 1576, Martin Frobisher reached the southeast corner of Baffin Island. He found a great bay that he named after himself. He thought it was the mouth of the route to China.

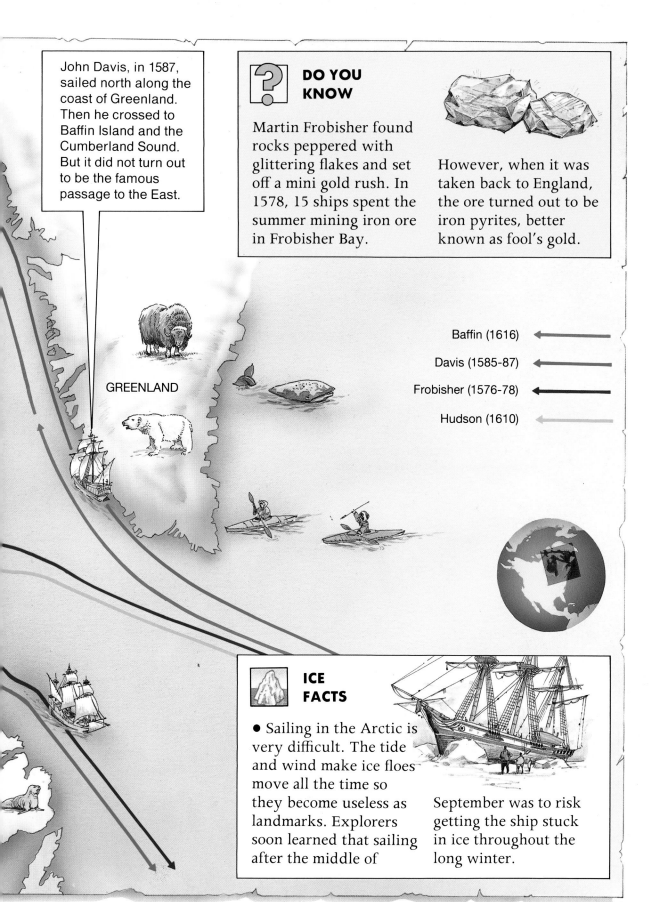

John Davis, in 1587, sailed north along the coast of Greenland. Then he crossed to Baffin Island and the Cumberland Sound. But it did not turn out to be the famous passage to the East.

? DO YOU KNOW

Martin Frobisher found rocks peppered with glittering flakes and set off a mini gold rush. In 1578, 15 ships spent the summer mining iron ore in Frobisher Bay.

However, when it was taken back to England, the ore turned out to be iron pyrites, better known as fool's gold.

GREENLAND

Baffin (1616)

Davis (1585-87)

Frobisher (1576-78)

Hudson (1610)

ICE FACTS

● Sailing in the Arctic is very difficult. The tide and wind make ice floes move all the time so they become useless as landmarks. Explorers soon learned that sailing after the middle of September was to risk getting the ship stuck in ice throughout the long winter.

Who were the conquistadores?

The conquistadores were soldier-explorers from Spain and Portugal. They arrived in America hard on the heels of the first explorers and set about attacking the natives and taking their lands. They raided far and wide for treasure, captured Indian towns and converted the survivors to Christianity.

Within fifty years, they had established the rule of Spain and Portugal all across South and Central America.

DO YOU KNOW

In 1532, Francisco Pizarro landed in Peru with only 180 soldiers and 37 horsemen. He found the Inca Empire in the midst of a bloody civil war.

Pizarro took the Inca prince Atahualpa prisoner. As ransom, the Incas offered to fill a room with gold and silver treasure to the height of a man.

But Atahualpa was never released. A few months later the Spaniards, tired of waiting for the ransom, executed him. Very swiftly after that, the Inca Empire fell apart.

2 King Montezuma let Cortés into the capital Tenochtitlan. The Spanish force of 500 soldiers did not seem threatening.

1 In February 1519, the conquistador Hernán Cortés led an army from Cuba to Mexico to attack the Empire of the Aztecs.

3 The city amazed the Spaniards. It had paved streets and sewers, and huge stone temples filled with treasure.

5 In 1521, helped by a smallpox epidemic, the Aztec capital fell to Cortés. Within a few years the Aztec Empire was replaced by a settlement known as New Spain.

4 The Aztecs were at the height of their powers at this time. Their armies were well organized and their soldiers were ferocious fighters.

Aztecs and Incas

The Aztecs ruled from Tenochtitlan, Mexico. The Inca capital was at Cuzco, Peru, South America.

Who explored Siberia?

The biggest country in the world is Russia, and the biggest region in it is Siberia. For many years it was a vast blank space on maps. It was in the 1550s, under Tsar Ivan the Terrible, that the first Cossack soldiers set off to explore Siberia. But the Cossacks were not good explorers because they never kept records or maps. It was not until 150 years later that Siberia was properly mapped and explored by Vitus Bering.

DO YOU KNOW

The Cossacks were bands of soldiers who elected their own war chiefs and hired themselves out to fight for whoever they chose. They brought most of western Siberia under Russian control in the 1600s.

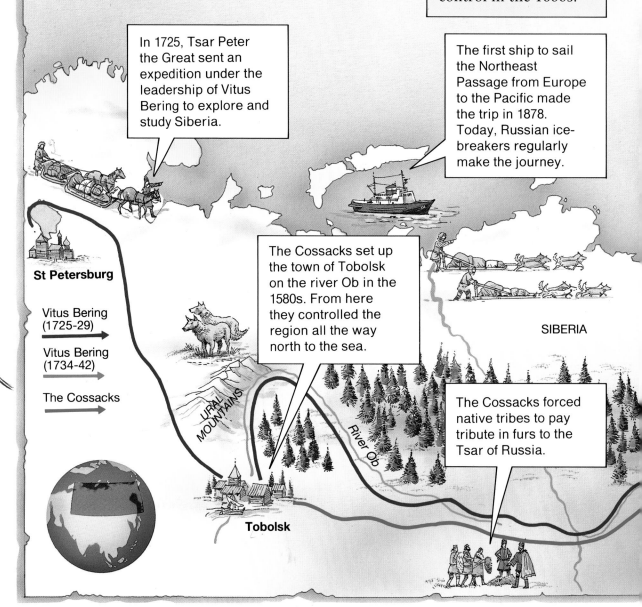

In 1725, Tsar Peter the Great sent an expedition under the leadership of Vitus Bering to explore and study Siberia.

The first ship to sail the Northeast Passage from Europe to the Pacific made the trip in 1878. Today, Russian ice-breakers regularly make the journey.

The Cossacks set up the town of Tobolsk on the river Ob in the 1580s. From here they controlled the region all the way north to the sea.

SIBERIA

St Petersburg

Vitus Bering (1725-29)

Vitus Bering (1734-42)

The Cossacks

URAL MOUNTAINS

River Ob

The Cossacks forced native tribes to pay tribute in furs to the Tsar of Russia.

Tobolsk

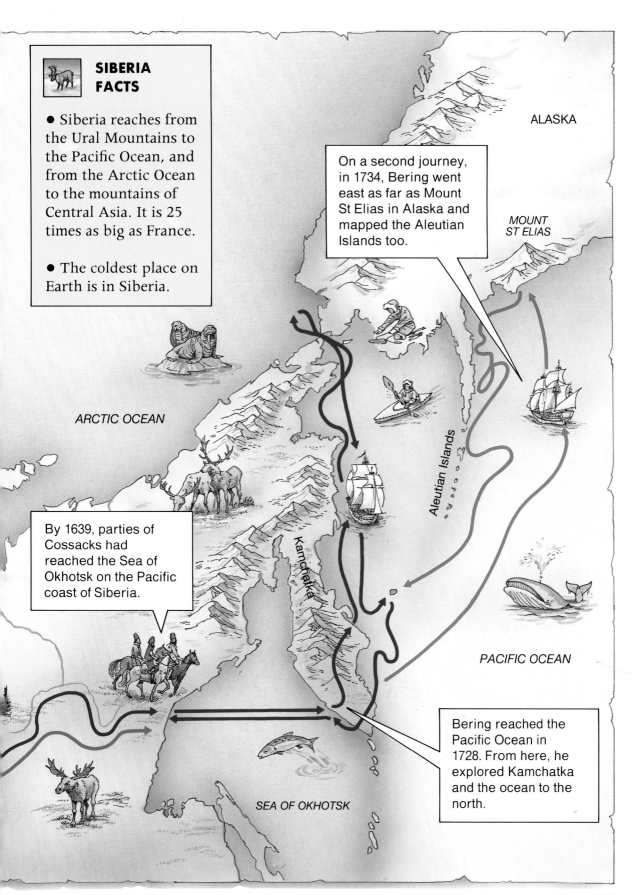

SIBERIA FACTS

• Siberia reaches from the Ural Mountains to the Pacific Ocean, and from the Arctic Ocean to the mountains of Central Asia. It is 25 times as big as France.

• The coldest place on Earth is in Siberia.

ALASKA

On a second journey, in 1734, Bering went east as far as Mount St Elias in Alaska and mapped the Aleutian Islands too.

MOUNT ST ELIAS

ARCTIC OCEAN

Aleutian Islands

Kamchatka

By 1639, parties of Cossacks had reached the Sea of Okhotsk on the Pacific coast of Siberia.

PACIFIC OCEAN

Bering reached the Pacific Ocean in 1728. From here, he explored Kamchatka and the ocean to the north.

SEA OF OKHOTSK

Who explored the biggest ocean?

The biggest ocean, by far, is the Pacific. All the continents in the world could fit into it with plenty of room to spare.

Captain James Cook is its most famous explorer. He sailed from England in 1768 on the first of three great voyages, during which he discovered New Zealand, mapped the coast of eastern Australia, and plotted the position of countless Pacific Islands. His ship carried scientists and artists who collected and sketched the animals and plants that they saw.

Sailors who spent weeks at sea without fresh food often got sick with a disease called scurvy. Cook attacked the problem with a diet of lemon and orange juice, vinegar, malt and sauerkraut (a cabbage dish). Men who wouldn't eat it were flogged.

Cook's ship in 1768 was the *Endeavour*. It had a crew of 100 and 15 months' food supply. It had space for lots of animal and plant specimens.

Cook's Travels

From 1768 to 1779 Cook charted the Pacific. In the south he mapped New Zealand, the east of Australia and the Pacific Islands. In the north he mapped as far as Alaska.

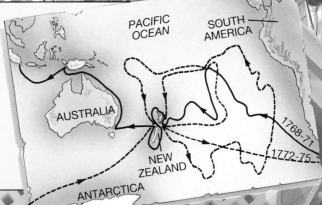

PACIFIC OCEAN
SOUTH AMERICA
AUSTRALIA
NEW ZEALAND
ANTARCTICA
1768-71
1772-75

Artists came back with sketches of the varied animals, people and places that the ship visited.

Cook was the first sailor to sail with a chronometer. This accurate clock helped him to work out longitude at sea.

Because they were badly mapped, the same islands had been found again and again. Cook now plotted them accurately.

The *Endeavour* was Cook's first ship. It was a 29-metre coaling ship, solidly built, spacious, and ideal for spending many months at sea.

HOME-MADE COMPASS

Using navigational tools such as a compass and a chronometer, Cook was able to plot the position of the Pacific Islands much more accurately than anybody had ever done before.

1 To make your own compass, stroke a needle along one end of a magnet several times.

2 Tie thread around the needle so it can swing freely. When it stops, it will be pointing North.

Where was the lost city of Timbuktu?

On the banks of the river Niger, at the edge of the Sahara Desert, lies the city of Timbuktu. Once it was the capital of a wealthy but little known desert kingdom. Because Europeans were banned from it, Timbuktu was a city of mystery. The first European explorer to go there was René Caillié in 1828. To get in, he disguised himself as an Egyptian Muslim. On his return he won a 10,000 franc prize for his exploits from the Paris Geographical Society.

The Sahara Desert

The Sahara covers one third of Africa and is the biggest desert in the world. Most of it is a stony plain, but some parts are covered in dunes of windblown sand which make it very difficult to travel across.

Timbuktu's tall towers and one-storey houses were built out of earth and sun-dried brick.

SAHARA DESERT

•Timbuktu

Nile

AFRICA

Caillié found a town in decay. What had once been a rich city, with palaces, wealthy merchants, and a busy trade in gold, had fallen to Morocco in 1591 and been left to decline.

Caillié, and later explorers, showed the Sahara could be crossed by travelling in camel caravans, following ancient trade routes.

Where is the source of the river Nile?

The river Nile is the main river to flow from Lake Victoria. From there it makes its way north, through Sudan and Egypt, to the Mediterranean Sea. It is the longest river in the world. Until the mid 1800s its source was a mystery. Explorers from Europe raced each other to be the first to find it.

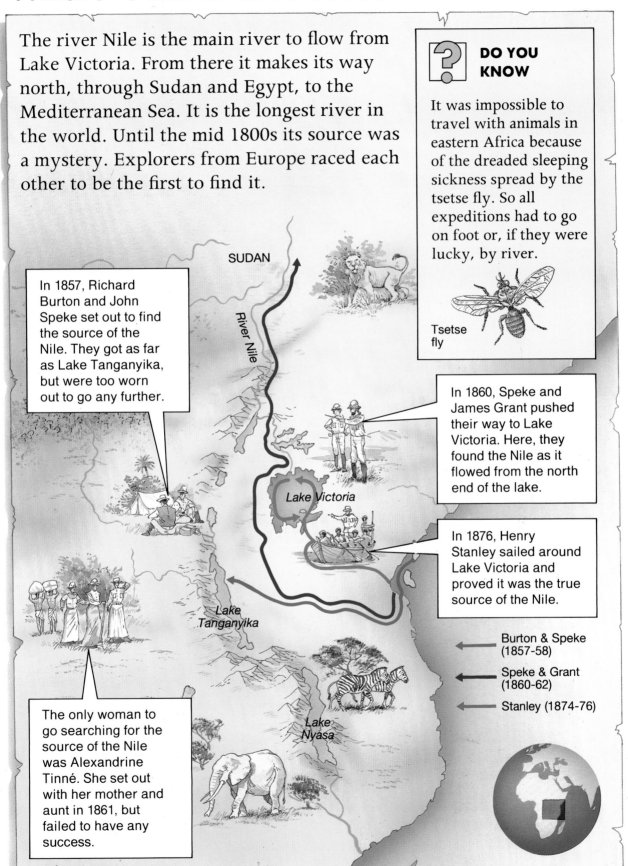

? DO YOU KNOW

It was impossible to travel with animals in eastern Africa because of the dreaded sleeping sickness spread by the tsetse fly. So all expeditions had to go on foot or, if they were lucky, by river.

Tsetse fly

SUDAN

River Nile

In 1857, Richard Burton and John Speke set out to find the source of the Nile. They got as far as Lake Tanganyika, but were too worn out to go any further.

In 1860, Speke and James Grant pushed their way to Lake Victoria. Here, they found the Nile as it flowed from the north end of the lake.

Lake Victoria

In 1876, Henry Stanley sailed around Lake Victoria and proved it was the true source of the Nile.

Lake Tanganyika

Burton & Speke (1857-58)

Speke & Grant (1860-62)

Stanley (1874-76)

Lake Nyasa

The only woman to go searching for the source of the Nile was Alexandrine Tinné. She set out with her mother and aunt in 1861, but failed to have any success.

31

Who said 'Doctor Livingstone, I presume?'

The most famous words in the history of exploration were spoken by Henry Stanley as he met David Livingstone beside Lake Tanganyika on 28 October 1871.

Livingstone was the most famous explorer of his day. In 1866 he travelled to Africa to help clear up disagreements about the source of the Nile. By 1871, nothing had been heard from him for several years. Many people began to fear he was dead. So the *New York Herald* newspaper sent Stanley, a reporter, to try to find him.

Stanley soon fell in love with exploring Africa. He organized his trips like military expeditions and sent back regular reports of his successful missions.

Livingstone was sick with fever by the time Stanley found him. Only two years later, in 1873, he died near Lake Bangweiku.

DO YOU KNOW

When Livingstone first arrived in South Africa in 1841 it was to be a missionary. It was only in order to carry the Christian gospel to the interior that he turned himself into an explorer.

Livingstone's Travels

Livingstone was world famous as the first known person to cross Africa. It took him from 1853 to 1856, and he travelled most of the way on foot.

Stanley travelled with an army of porters to carry tents, clothes and guns, and the cloth and beads that he needed to buy food and to impress local chiefs.

DO YOU KNOW

Stanley explored the Congo River with the help of a 12-metre-long collapsible steel boat called the *Lady Alice*. This heavy boat was lugged overland about 3000 km before being sailed down river a further 6400 km.

The *Lady Alice*

Stanley's boat was named after his fiancée

Who first crossed Australia?

The first expedition to cross Australia from south to north was a camel caravan in 1860, led by Robert Burke and William Wills.

Europeans first reached Australia in the 1600s. The coastal areas were settled by the British after 1788. But even as late as the 1850s, no settlers had any clear idea what lay at the heart of the continent, although plenty of Aborigines did.

? DO YOU KNOW

There were about 350,000 Aborigines in Australia when the first settlers arrived in 1788. They had been there 40,000 years. The Aborigines lived in around 700 tribes and spoke many different languages.

Ayers Rock

? DO YOU KNOW

As the heat and the lack of water at the heart of the continent became better known, explorers took to using camels instead of horses. The camels were so well suited to the land that today herds of their descendants run wild in the outback.

GULF OF
CARPENTARIA

4 In February 1861, they reached the Gulf of Carpentaria, having made the first south-north crossing of Australia.

3 Burke, Wills and two others rode north on camels towards the sea. This was the first time camels were used to explore the outback.

GREAT DIVIDING RANGE

Cooper Creek

5 Three exhausted men (one had already died) got back to Cooper Creek in April, only to find that the others had given up waiting. Burke and Wills died. The third man, King, was helped by Aborigines and he survived.

2 In November, the expedition split into two groups. Three men stayed at Cooper Creek with a store of supplies to await the return of the others.

River Darling

River Murray

● **Menindee**

1 An expedition of seven set out from Melbourne in August 1860, heading for Cooper Creek.

● **Melbourne**

Who climbed highest?

Two men became famous in 1953 for climbing higher than anyone had ever done before. They were Edmund Hillary and Tenzing Norgay. On 29 May, they reached the summit of Everest, the highest mountain in the world. Standing at the top, they were over 8.8 kilometres above sea-level.

 DO YOU KNOW

The deepest anyone has ever travelled under the sea is almost 11 km. In 1960, Jacques Picard and Don Walsh took their special diving ship, the *Trieste*, to the bottom of the Marianas Trench in the Pacific Ocean. This is the deepest place on Earth. Even Mount Everest would be swallowed up without a trace here.

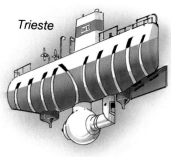
Trieste

Everest is very difficult to climb because of its steepness, strong winds and thin air.

 WHAT SHAPE IS A SLOPE?

By looking at maps, mountaineers can tell what shape a mountain slope will be. To see for yourself, look at the circular lines called contour lines on a map.

 1

 2

If the lines are close together at the summit, the upper slope is very steep and the mountain will be like diagram 1.

If the lines are close together at the bottom, the mountain has a flatter top and will be like diagram 2.

Who first went into Space?

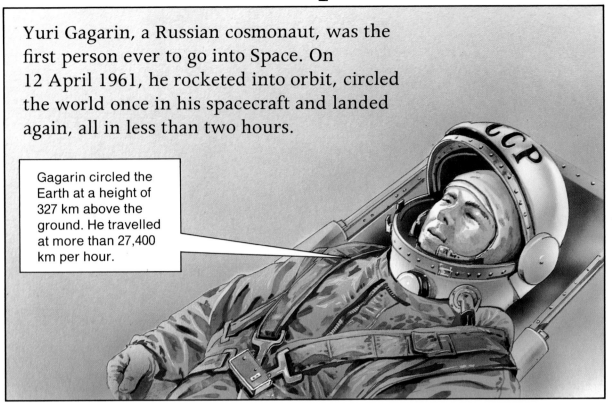

Yuri Gagarin, a Russian cosmonaut, was the first person ever to go into Space. On 12 April 1961, he rocketed into orbit, circled the world once in his spacecraft and landed again, all in less than two hours.

Gagarin circled the Earth at a height of 327 km above the ground. He travelled at more than 27,400 km per hour.

How far have people gone into Space?

The farthest from Earth anyone has ever travelled is the 400,000 kilometre trip to the Moon. Between 1969 and 1972, the United States sent six missions there.

? DO YOU KNOW

Space probes without people in them have been sent farther than the Moon to explore deep into Space.

The first astronaut to set a moonboot on to the Moon was Neil Armstrong on 21 July 1969.

Who first reached the North Pole?

The first person to stand at the North Pole was Robert Peary, an American Navy officer. In 1909, on his third attempt, he left his ship in the ice off Ellesmere Island and set out on foot. His team of 17 included a dozen Inuit, 12 sledges and 133 dogs. On 6 April, a small six-man advance party finally reached its goal.

DO YOU KNOW

In 1911, two expeditions raced each other to become the first to reach the South Pole. The Norwegians, led by Roald Amundsen, used dogs to haul their supplies and arrived at the Pole first.

The British, under Robert Scott, had to haul their own sledges after their ponies collapsed. All five exhausted men died returning from the South Pole.

Of the six men to reach the North Pole, four were Inuit.

Amundsen
Scott

SOUTH POLE

Peary couldn't have made it without using Inuit survival skills. He wore snowshoes, wrapped up in animal furs, and used dogs to pull the sledges.

Useful words

Aborigine   The first people who lived in a country, especially the first Australians.

Chronometer   A very accurate clock used to measure longitude at sea or in the air.

Conquistador   A Spanish soldier-explorer of the 1500s.

Contour line   A line on a map joining points of equal height. The shape of a mountain can be estimated by looking at its contour lines on a map.

Cosmonaut   The Russian word for an explorer of Space.

Continent   Continents are large areas of land, and the Earth has seven of them – Africa, Antarctica, Asia, Oceania, Europe, North America and South America.

Equator   An imaginary line around the Earth, halfway between the North and South poles.

Indians   The native people of America and India.

Inuit   The native people of Greenland, Canada and Northern Alaska.

Latitude and longitude   Lines of latitude and longitude are drawn on maps to help show the position of places accurately. Latitude lines run from East to West, and longitude lines run from North to South.

Missionary   A person who goes to another country to tell people about his or her religion and to do helpful work.

Mountaineer   A person who climbs mountains.

Navigator   The person who works out the direction for a ship or aircraft.

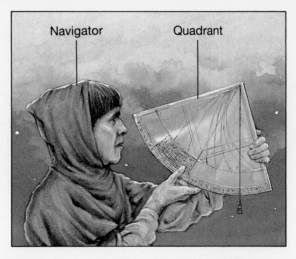

Navigator   Quadrant

Quadrant   A navigational instrument used for working out latitude.

Orbit   The path followed by a body in Space around another body. A spacecraft orbits the Earth, for example.

Scurvy   A disease caused by a diet lacking in fresh vegetables.

Tsar   The Emperor of Russia.

Tsetse fly   A fly found in tropical Africa which spreads the disease sleeping sickness.

Tsetse fly

Vikings   Scandinavian seafarers who travelled across many countries between the 700s and 1100s.

Index